Mrs (

Francis Frith's
Chelmsford

Photographic Memories

Francis Frith's Chelmsford

Russell Thompson

First published in the United Kingdom in 2001 by
Frith Book Company Ltd

Paperback Edition 2001
ISBN 1-85937-310-0

British Library Cataloguing in Publication Data

Francis Frith's Chelmsford
Russell Thompson

Frith Book Company Ltd
Frith's Barn, Teffont,
Salisbury, Wiltshire SP3 5QP
Tel: +44 (0) 1722 716 376
Email: info@francisfrith.co.uk
www.francisfrith.co.uk

Printed and bound in Great Britain

Front Cover: Chelmsford, High Street 1919 69010

AS WITH ANY HISTORICAL DATABASE THE FRITH ARCHIVE IS CONSTANTLY BEING CORRECTED AND IMPROVED AND THE PUBLISHERS WOULD WELCOME INFORMATION ON OMISSIONS OR INACCURACIES

Contents

Francis Frith: *Victorian Pioneer*

FRANCIS FRITH, Victorian founder of the world-famous photographic archive, was a complex and multi-talented man. A devout Quaker and a highly successful Victorian businessman, he was both philosophic by nature and pioneering in outlook.

By 1855 Francis Frith had already established a wholesale grocery business in Liverpool, and sold it for the astonishing sum of £200,000, which is the equivalent today of over £15,000,000. Now a multi-millionaire, he was able to indulge his passion for travel. As a child he had pored over travel books written by early explorers, and his fancy and imagination had been stirred by family holidays to the sublime mountain regions of Wales and Scotland. 'What a land of spirit-stirring and enriching scenes and places!' he had written. He was to return to these scenes of grandeur in later years to 'recapture the thousands of vivid and tender memories', but with a different purpose. Now in his thirties, and captivated by the new science of photography, Frith set out on a series of pioneering journeys to the Nile regions that occupied him from 1856 until 1860.

Intrigue and Adventure

He took with him on his travels a specially-designed wicker carriage that acted as both dark-room and sleeping chamber. These far-flung journeys were packed with intrigue and adventure. In his life story, written when he was sixty-three, Frith tells of being held captive by bandits, and of fighting 'an awful midnight battle to the very point of surrender with a deadly pack of hungry, wild dogs'. Sporting flowing Arab costume, Frith arrived at Akaba by camel seventy years before Lawrence, where he encountered 'desert princes and rival sheikhs, blazing with jewel-hilted swords'.

During these extraordinary adventures he was assiduously exploring the desert regions bordering the Nile and patiently recording the antiquities and peoples with his camera. He was the first photographer to venture beyond the sixth cataract. Africa was still the mysterious 'Dark Continent', and Stanley and Livingstone's historic meeting was a decade into the future. The conditions for picture taking confound belief. He laboured for hours in his wicker dark-room in the sweltering heat of the desert, while the volatile chemicals fizzed dangerously in their trays. Often he was forced to work in remote tombs and caves where conditions were cooler. Back in London he exhibited his photographs and was 'rapturously cheered' by members of the Royal Society. His reputation as a photographer was made overnight. An eminent modern historian has likened their impact on the population of the time to that on our own generation of the first photographs taken on the surface of the moon.

Venture of a Life-Time

Characteristically, Frith quickly spotted the opportunity to create a new business as a specialist publisher of photographs. He lived in an era of immense and sometimes violent change. For the poor in the early part of Victoria's reign work was a drudge and the hours long, and people had precious little free time to enjoy themselves. Most had no transport other than a cart or gig at their disposal, and had not travelled far beyond the boundaries of their own town or village. However, by the 1870s, the railways had threaded their way across the country, and Bank Holidays and half-day Saturdays had been made obligatory by Act of Parliament. All of a sudden the ordinary working man and his family were able to enjoy days out and see a little more of the world.

With characteristic business acumen, Francis Frith foresaw that these new tourists would enjoy having souvenirs to commemorate their days out. In 1860 he married Mary Ann Rosling and set out with the intention of photographing every city, town and village in Britain. For the next thirty years he travelled the country by train and by pony and trap, producing fine photographs of seaside resorts and beauty spots that were keenly bought by millions of Victorians. These prints were painstakingly pasted into family albums and pored over during the dark nights of winter, rekindling precious memories of summer excursions.

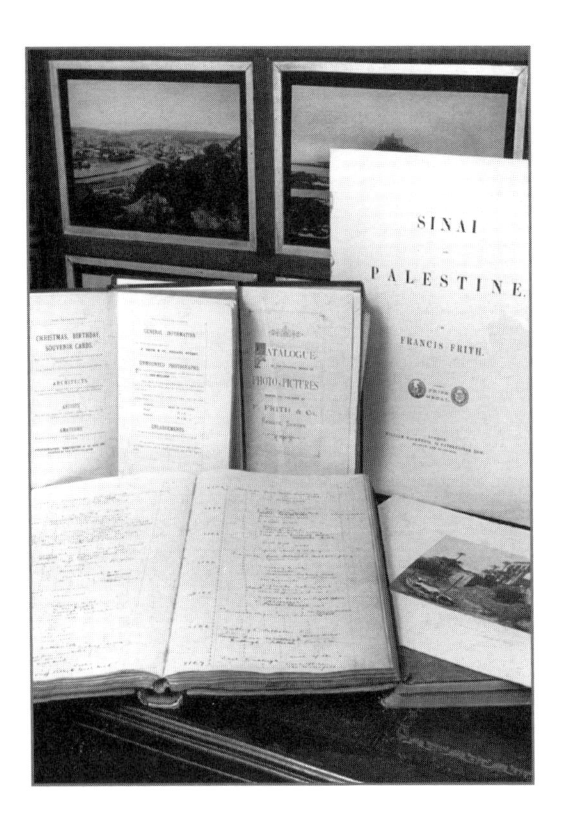

The Rise of Frith & Co

Frith's studio was soon supplying retail shops all over the country. To meet the demand he gathered about him a small team of photographers, and published the work of independent artist-photographers of the calibre of Roger Fenton and Francis Bedford. In order to gain some understanding of the scale of Frith's business one only has to look at the catalogue issued by Frith & Co in 1886: it runs to some 670 pages, listing not only many thousands of views of the British Isles but also many photographs of most European countries, and China, Japan, the USA and Canada – note the sample page shown above from the hand-written *Frith & Co* ledgers detailing pictures taken. By 1890 Frith had created the greatest specialist photographic publishing company in the world,

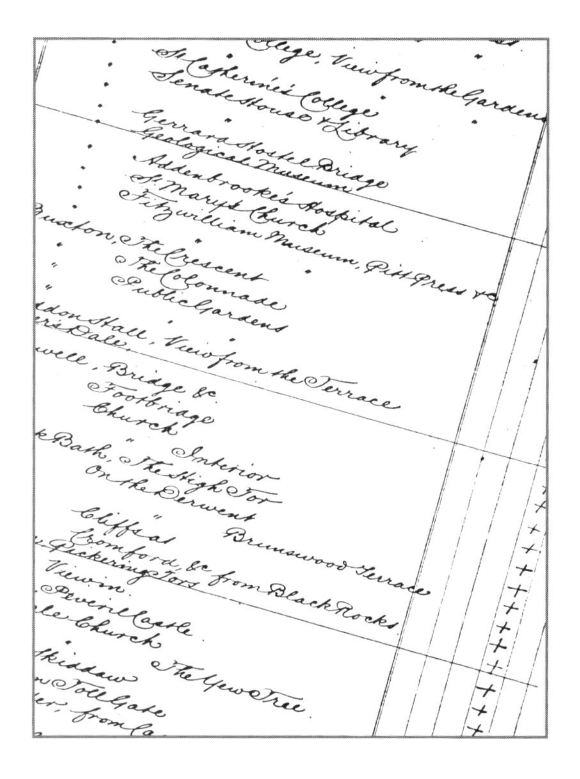

...llege, View from the Garden
St Catherine's College
Senate House & Library
Gerrard Hostel Bridge
Geological Museum
Addenbrooke's Hospital
St Mary's Church
Fitzwilliam Museum, Pitt Press &c
...ucton, The Crescent
The Colonnade
Public Gardens
...don Hall, View from the Terrace
...ri Dale
...well, Bridge &c.
Footbridge
Church
...k Bath, The High Tor
Interior
On the Derwent
Cliffs at
Brunswood Terrace
Bromford, &c from Black Rocks
...Pickering Tors
View in
Peveril Castle
...le Church
...kiddaw
The Yew Tree
...w Toll Gate
...er, from Ca...

with over 2,000 outlets – more than the combined number that Boots and WH Smith have today! The picture on the right shows the *Frith & Co* display board at Ingleton in the Yorkshire Dales. Beautifully constructed with mahogany frame and gilt inserts, it could display up to a dozen local scenes.

Postcard Bonanza

The ever-popular holiday postcard we know today took many years to develop. In 1870 the Post Office issued the first plain cards, with a pre-printed stamp on one face. In 1894 they allowed other publishers' cards to be sent through the mail with an attached adhesive halfpenny stamp. Demand grew rapidly, and in 1895 a new size of postcard was permitted called the court card, but there was little room for illustration. In 1899, a year after Frith's death, a new card measuring 5.5 x 3.5 inches became the standard format, but it was not until 1902 that the divided back came into being, with address and message on one face and a full-size illustration on the other. *Frith & Co* were in the vanguard of postcard development, and Frith's sons Eustace and Cyril continued their father's monumental task, expanding the number of views offered to the public and recording more and more places in Britain, as the coasts and countryside were opened up to mass travel.

Francis Frith died in 1898 at his villa in Cannes, his great project still growing. The archive he created continued in business for another seventy years. By 1970 it contained over a third of a million pictures of 7,000 cities, towns and villages. The massive photographic record Frith has left to us stands as a living monument to a special and very remarkable man.

Frith's Archive: *A Unique Legacy*

Francis Frith's legacy to us today is of immense significance and value, for the magnificent archive of evocative photographs he created provides a unique record of change in 7,000 cities, towns and villages throughout Britain over a century and more. Frith and his fellow studio photographers revisited locations many times down the years to update their views, compiling for us an enthralling and colourful pageant of British life and character.

We tend to think of Frith's sepia views of Britain as nostalgic, for most of us use them to conjure up memories of places in our own lives with which we have family associations. It often makes us forget that to Francis Frith they were records of daily life as it was actually being lived in the cities, towns and villages of his day. The Victorian age was one of great and often bewildering change for ordinary people, and though the pictures evoke an impression of slower times, life was as busy and hectic as it is today.

We are fortunate that Frith was a photographer of the people, dedicated to recording the minutiae of everyday life. For it is this sheer wealth of visual data, the painstaking chronicle of changes in dress, transport, street layouts, buildings, housing, engineering and landscape that captivates us so much today. His remarkable images offer us a powerful link with the past and with the lives of our ancestors.

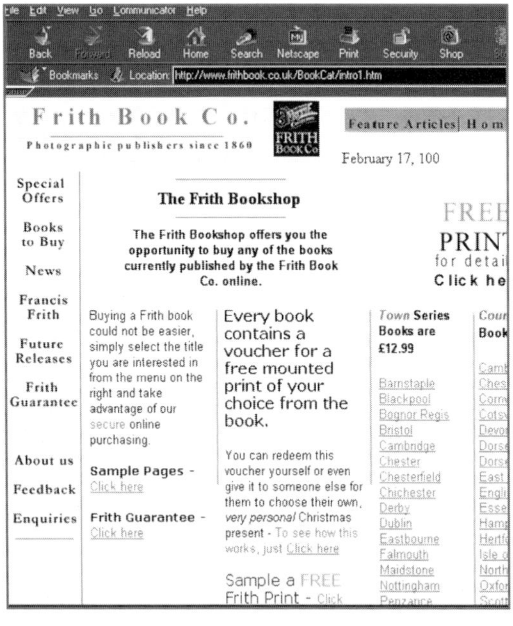

See Frith at www. frithbook.co.uk

Today's Technology

Computers have now made it possible for Frith's many thousands of images to be accessed almost instantly. In the Frith archive today, each photograph is carefully 'digitised' then stored on a CD Rom. Frith archivists can locate a single photograph amongst thousands within seconds. Views can be catalogued and sorted under a variety of categories of place and content to the immediate benefit of researchers.

Inexpensive reference prints can be created for them at the touch of a mouse button, and a wide range of books and other printed materials assembled and published for a wider, more general readership - in the next twelve months over a hundred Frith local history titles will be published! The day-to-day workings of the archive are very different from how they were in Francis Frith's time: imagine the herculean task of sorting through eleven tons of glass negatives as Frith had to do to locate a particular sequence of pictures! Yet the archive still prides itself on maintaining the same high standards of excellence laid down by Francis Frith, including the painstaking cataloguing and indexing of every view.

It is curious to reflect on how the internet now allows researchers in America and elsewhere greater instant access to the archive than Frith himself ever enjoyed. Many thousands of individual views can be called up on screen within seconds on one of the Frith internet sites, enabling people living continents away to revisit the streets of their ancestral home town, or view places in Britain where they have enjoyed holidays. Many overseas researchers welcome the chance to view special theme selections, such as transport, sports, costume and ancient monuments.

We are certain that Francis Frith would have heartily approved of these modern developments in imaging techniques, for he himself was always working at the very limits of Victorian photographic technology.

The Value of the Archive Today

Because of the benefits brought by the computer, Frith's images are increasingly studied by social historians, by researchers into genealogy and ancestory, by architects, town planners, and by teachers and schoolchildren involved in local history projects.

In addition, the archive offers every one of us an opportunity to examine the places where we and our families have lived and worked down the years. Highly successful in Frith's own era, the archive is now, a century and more on, entering a new phase of popularity.

The Past in Tune with the Future

Historians consider the Francis Frith Collection to be of prime national importance. It is the only archive of its kind remaining in private ownership and has been valued at a million pounds. However, this figure is now rapidly increasing as digital technology enables more and more people around the world to enjoy its benefits.

Francis Frith's archive is now housed in an historic timber barn in the beautiful village of Teffont in Wiltshire. Its founder would not recognize the archive office as it is today. In place of the many thousands of dusty boxes containing glass plate negatives and an all-pervading odour of photographic chemicals, there are now ranks of computer screens. He would be amazed to watch his images travelling round the world at unimaginable speeds through network and internet lines.

The archive's future is both bright and exciting. Francis Frith, with his unshakeable belief in making photographs available to the greatest number of people, would undoubtedly approve of what is being done today with his lifetime's work. His photographs, depicting our shared past, are now bringing pleasure and enlightenment to millions around the world a century and more after his death.

Chelmsford - *An Introduction*

NOT EVERYBODY LIKES Chelmsford, it is true. When the young Charles Dickens stayed there in 1835, he found it "the dullest and most stupid spot on the face of the Earth". His main complaint was that none of the shops sold Sunday papers!

Chelmsfordians know different, though not all of them would care to admit it. It is a town that has been through many incarnations - market town, coaching town, industrial town, shopping town. For this reason it frequently seems to be a town in transition.

The photographs in this book chart some of the changes Chelmsford has been through: horse-drawn vehicles vanishing in the face of bicycles, and then cars; the loss of old timber-framed shops; brave new civic buildings sprouting up in their place. Some fixtures seem to be ever-present - the Stone Bridge, for example - while elsewhere an inn becomes a church, and the church becomes a supermarket, all in the space of a few decades.

This is very much a feature of Chelmsford - and it is a criticism constantly levelled against it: the failure to preserve its oldest and most interesting buildings. It is true that much has been lost in recent years - Tindal Street, the Corn Exchange, the Friars - and that a lot of the newer architecture is, to put it mildly, lacking in appeal.

There is a famous map of Chelmsford, drawn in 1591 by John Walker, in which every shop and tenement is faithfully depicted. It is a place of timbered gables, square courtyards, and chimneys like little red hammer-heads. There is almost nothing that is recognisable today, except the familiar shape of the High Street - wide at the top, and narrowing as it sweeps over the bridge into Moulsham; and the way the two rivers, the Can and the Chelmer, hold the town in their V-shaped clinch. So, even today, there is an older Chelmsford to be seen, it is just that sometimes you have to use your imagination.

The earliest of these photographs capture the town at a time of immense civic pride. It had become a borough in 1888. This was of very great importance: contemporary pictures show a sea of proud townspeople clamouring round the Corn Exchange on the day the Charter of Incorporation arrived from London. Interestingly enough, there are similar plans afoot, at the time of writing, for Chelmsford to be granted the status of a city. It all comes round again, as they say.

For much of the 19th century, though, Chelmsford had been trying to pull itself up by the bootlaces: the upmarket development of New London Road, with its churches, infirmary and townhouses, had begun in 1839; four years later, the railway had steamed into town on an enormous red-brick viaduct. A Board of Health had been busy building a waterworks, opening a cemetery and relocating the livestock market. Soon after Chelmsford's incorporation, the town acquired its Recreation Ground: an expanse of fields and water-meadows were laid-out with paths, flowerbeds, bridges and bowling greens. Not far away, there were nonconformist churches and literary institutes appearing almost overnight. In 1914 St Mary's church achieved new status: a plucky little cathedral at the hub of England's largest diocese.

However, to find Chelmsford's architectural heyday, it is usual to focus on the contributions of John Johnson, the County Surveyor in the late 1700s: his were the Shire Hall and the Stone Bridge - still two of Chelmsford's most recognisable features. He also rebuilt the church after its roof fell in.

The Stone Bridge serves to remind us that Chelmsford's origins were water-related. A Roman encampment had been established at the point where the London-Colchester road bridged the River Can. After a while, it developed into a small town called Caesaromagus - Caesar's plain - the only town in Britain to bear Caesar's name. It had shops, a temple and a bathhouse. Everything had crumbled away, however, by the time the Saxons arrived - even the bridge. The new settlers avoided settling on the old site, preferring the higher ground near what is now Rectory Lane. Nevertheless, there was one particular East Saxon - a man called Ceolmaer - who was in some way connected with a ford across the smaller of the two local rivers. At any rate, he gave his name to it: Ceolmaer's ford - Chelmsford. It seems to have been a notorious crossing-point.

The Can was given a new bridge in 1100 and the through-traffic, which had been making a detour through Writtle for several centuries, was able to pass this way again. But there was still no town yet. It was not until 1199 that Chelmsford was granted a market: this was to occur once a week, on Fridays. A triangular market place appeared, the market-stalls became permanent shops, and a church was built to serve the new community. Chelmsford's buildings met Moulsham's at the bridge – it is important to remember that this has always been a town of two halves.

The new settlement seemed to have a certain kudos. It made a good stop-over point for courtiers on royal business; its central position meant it was a convenient place for Essex's assizes to be held; and at some point a friary was established in Moulsham. By the mid 13th century, Chelmsford was the county town.

So it has remained, though it has always had its detractors. Chelmsford has simply learnt to weather the unfavourable write-ups in guide-books, and the gentle lampooning by television comedians. It has suffered, certainly, from sharing a bed with Colchester - arguably the most historically interesting town in Britain.

Chelmsford is not a large place by any means, but then Essex, despite its high population, has never been a county of big towns. Nor is Chelmsford a glamorous place, because for the past hundred years at least, its prime concerns have been industrial. We should not forget that Chelmsford was the first town in Britain to install electric streetlamps (albeit briefly), or that it was the cradle of radio-broadcasting; and, indeed, of ball-bearing manufacture. Let's hear it for Crompton's, Marconi's and Hoffman's - Chelmsford's 'big three' engineering firms.

This book also contains pictures of some of Chelmsford's outlying villages. These have been arranged as if we are following a wide clockwise arc around the county town. Some of these outliers had already been engulfed by Chelmsford at the start of the 20th century, but it is true to say that they still retain their own characteristics: Springfield with its mill and canal-basin; Great Baddow with its majestic church; Writtle with its duck-pond, village-green and timber-framed houses. Danbury and Little Baddow figure here, too: parishes of heathlands, woods, and surprising hills. On the opposite side of Chelmsford stands Pleshey, a curious village built inside the ramparts of a long-collapsed castle. Completing the tour are Great and Little Waltham - hardy thoroughfare settlements that have become quiet backwaters since acquiring their bypasses.

History is a peculiar thing. Like nature, it can be extremely cruel: all too often, there is a 'dog-eat-dogness' about it - a quality that is particularly pronounced in Chelmsford. The old gives way to the new, and it is for this reason that Chelmsford, for better or for worse, is always 'of its time'. Right now, it seems to be reinventing itself as a town of plazas, riverside walks, and shopping experiences. Good luck to it. Elsewhere, along Wharf Road, a new county record office has recently opened which is widely regarded as the best in the country and, love it or loathe it, there is the annual 'V' festival in Hylands Park. People are hearing of Chelmsford, who had never heard of it before.

Outside Loveday's, the long-established jeweller's at Baddow Road corner, there is a sculpture. It was unveiled in 1999 and is called 'Guardian Figures'. On one side there is a Roman centurion, on the other a Dominican friar. It is good to remember the pioneers. However, since this book concerns itself with photography, we shall, for the time being, concentrate on the last hundred years of Chelmsford's convoluted history. Remember - it may not have sold Sunday papers in 1835, but it really has got a lot going for it.

North of the Can: The Town Centre

Chelmsford
Broomfield Road 1925 78167

Anyone standing in this position today would be risking their life, to say the least. While the buildings at Broomfield Road corner date back to the 1840s, it was quite a while before the ribbon development crept further up. We are just beyond the Grammar School here, looking north.

Chelmsford
The Bus Station
c1955 C73045
Initially, Chelmsford's bus garage had been in one of the arches under the viaduct, but in 1918 the Bus Company acquired the adjacent timber-yard in Duke Street and has used the site ever since. The current building dates from 1937. Daniel Defoe had apparently once lived in a house that stood towards the centre of this photo.

▼ **Chelmsford, The Grammar School 1892** 31516
King Edward VI Grammar School - known as KEGS - was theoretically founded by that monarch in 1551. In fact, he was simply presenting a new charter to a church school that had existed since the 14th century. The Broomfield Road premises - pictured in the year of their completion - were the school's third proper home.

▼ **Chelmsford, Duke Street c1950** C73008
The left-hand side of Duke Street has not changed much since the 1950s, but the opposite side has. The building nearest to the camera, Rainsford House, was built around the turn of the century. Since 1924 it had housed the town's municipal offices, but was replaced in the 1960s by a new Civic Suite.

▲ **Chelmsford, The Civic Suite and War Memorial c1960** C73078
The building to the extreme left, with the bicycle against its balusters, was the public library until the late 1980s. Broomfield Road corner was already a problem, with its 'No Right Turn' signs and people wary of crossing the road. The snub-nosed vehicle on the right is a Scammell lorry - used extensively by British Rail.

◄ **Chelmsford**
The Public Library 1906

56890

Built in 1906, this was the town's library until 1935, when new premises were completed in Duke Street. Subsequently it became part of the School of Art and Technology (currently Anglia Polytechnic University). The Chelmsford & Essex Museum, too, was housed here before the more capacious Oaklands House became available in 1929.

SOUTHEND
12
HK8635

Chelmsford
Duke Street 1919
69017

The pub in the foreground is the Railway Tavern. A previous landlady, it is said, would only serve people who looked like railwaymen. We are, indeed, opposite the station here. Behind the trees is the Friends' Meeting House (built 1824). The tall chimney belongs to Wells & Perry's Chelmsford Brewery.

◄ **Chelmsford Duke Street 1906**

56883

Although it had decamped to Broomfield Road by the time this picture was taken, the Grammar School had formerly stood here - the entrance to the old buildings being just to the left of the Coach & Horses with its substantial sign. Further down, the shop with the clock and the 'eyes' was later removed in a road-widening scheme.

Chelmsford, Duke Street 1919 69015
The Lion & Lamb, on the left, backed right onto the Chelmsford Brewery. Today there is a new Lion & Lamb on the site (although it has recently been rechristened 'Main Street'). Here, looking up, both creatures can be seen in 3D, on the pediment. Judging by the hanging sign, it was already evident that people sensed the car was here to stay. Duke Street takes its name from Guy Duk, a 15th century landowner.

Chelmsford, St Mary's Church 1892 31510
St Mary's was never built to be a cathedral: until 1914 it was simply the parish church. A major rebuilding occurred in the 15th century, and much of the present structure dates from that time. The triangular tomb in the foreground commemorates "three unfortunate females" who died in a fire in the High Street in 1808.

Chelmsford, The Cathedral 1919 69022
When Chelmsford became the centre of a new diocese, it pipped several other applicants at the post: Barking, Colchester, Thaxted, Woodford, Waltham Abbey and West Ham were all disappointed. The church's dedication was changed to St Mary the Virgin, St Peter and St Cedd - the latter being a Northumbrian monk who had done early missionary work in Essex. The tall cross is in memory of Henry Johnson, rector here 1880-94.

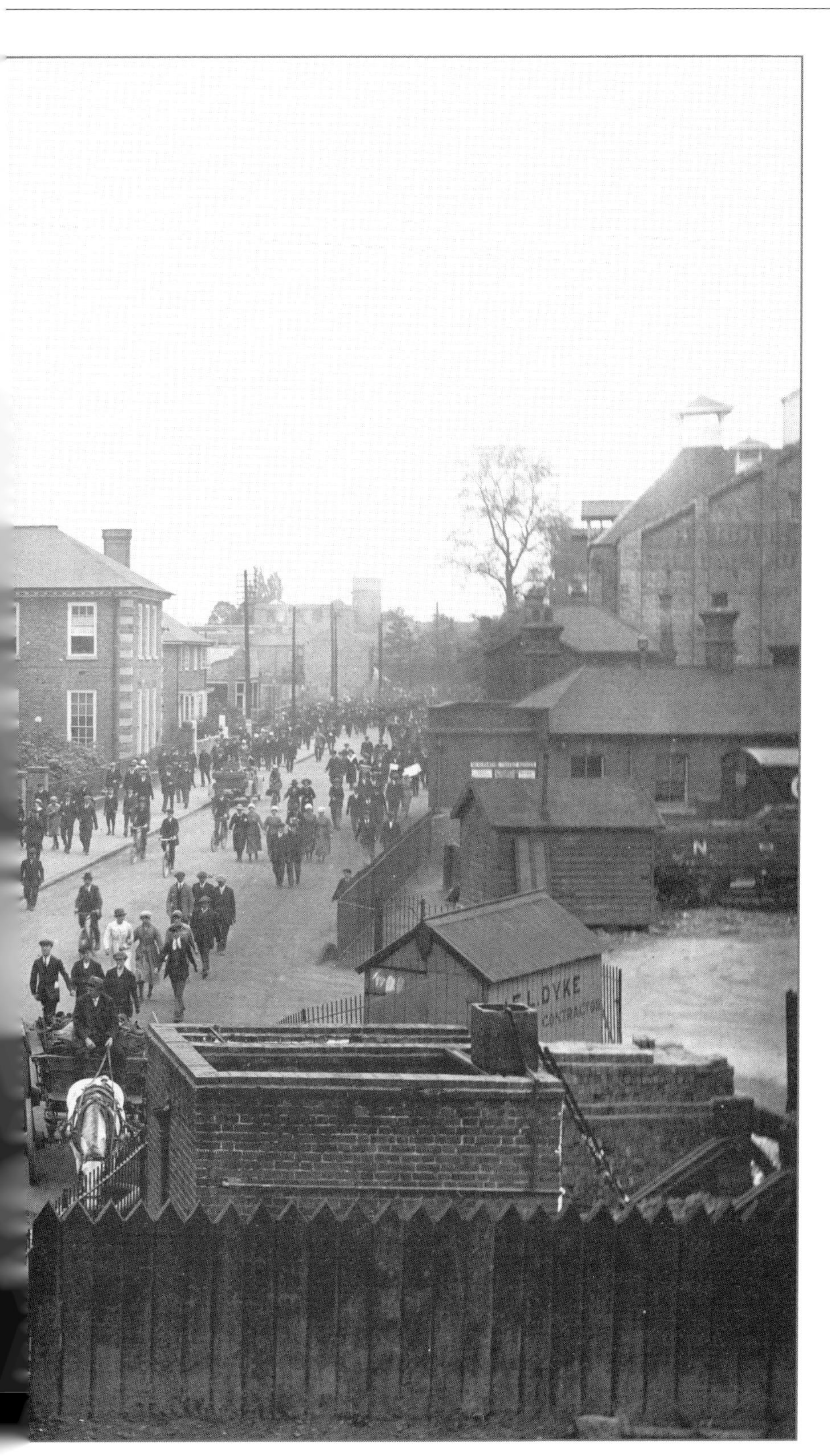

Chelmsford
The Marconi Works
1919 69028

Midday. The Marconi works had sprung up in 1912 opposite the goods yard and cattle pens belonging to the railway. Guglielmo Marconi had first established his firm in Chelmsford in 1899. Much of the workforce pictured here is probably actually coming from Hoffman's, the famous ball-bearing works further up the street.

Chelmsford, The Cathedral, Interior 1919 69024
One night in January 1800, the roof of St Mary's caved in, bringing sections of the walls down with it. Workmen had apparently loosened some of the pillars in preparing a vault. Services were held at the Shire Hall until the church was reopened in 1803. Any cracks visible in 1919 were, we hope, purely superficial.

Chelmsford, The Marconi Works c1955 C73041
Marconi's New Street factory was the first purpose-built radio-works in the world.When the previous premises - a former mill in Hall Street - became too cramped, this building was constructed on a former cricket field. New Street's first tentative radio broadcasts were made in 1920.

Chelmsford, Judge Tindal c1965 C73071

Chelmsford's most visible statue is that of Chief Justice Nicholas Conyngham Tindal (1776-1846). He was born in Moulsham Street, in the vicinity of what is now Lloyds TSB Bank. Erected in 1851 in the Square that bears his name, the statue was unceremoniously shifted a few years ago, in order to ease traffic-flow.

Chelmsford, The Shire Hall 1895 35515
Note the man with the roller, flattening the pathway: a necessary job in the days of dirt roads. Frederick Spalding's shop (photography and picture-framing) seems to be attracting a degree of interest. Next door is Henry Cleale's ironmongery, with the enamel bowls outside; in the foreground is James Wray's, drapers.

Chelmsford, The Shire Hall 1892 31507
The Shire Hall was built in 1789-91 by John Johnson, the County Surveyor. It is Chelmsford's most imposing public building. Over to the left are the studios of Frederick Spalding, the well-known photographer. His premises are capped with a lantern-like structure, to let in maximum light. He also traded in gifts and knick-knacks.

Chelmsford, The Shire Hall and Tindal Square 1895 35516
The three panels on the Shire Hall represent Wisdom, Mercy and Justice. In front is the Cannon: captured from Sebastopol during the Crimean War, it now stands in Oaklands Park. One night in 1907, a group of apprentices, intent on japery, actually fired a blank charge from it. The only casualty was a streetlamp.

Chelmsford, Tindal Square 1906 56881
To the forefront stands a horse-trough supplied by the RSPCA, and over to the right is one of the enterprises that would have kept the horses busy - Gilbey's Wines & Spirits, with its cart parked outside. The Chelmsford Window Cleaner was more self-sufficient: his handcart is just visible behind the Coal & Coke Merchants' shop.

◄ **Chelmsford**
The Shire Hall c1955

C73059

By the 1950s, it was becoming apparent that Chelmsford had a traffic problem: these Ford Consuls and Austin A35s, among others, had seen to that. The 'No Entry - One Way Street' signs were an attempt to effect a remedy. In the background, Barclay's Bank stands on a site already occupied by a bank in 1790.

◀ **Chelmsford, The Shire Hall 1919** 69021
The building with the cupola was Chelmsford's first purpose-built police station (erected in 1907), so the policeman in the picture was not far from home. His successors would stand in this same spot on points-duty. Note the car with its wheel-covers - a feature that was not phased out until the late 1920s.

▼ **Chelmsford, The Shire Hall c1965** C73070
Further attempts were being made to ease the road-congestion: a cluster of traffic lights, individual lanes, and 'Keep Left' signs. The Mini and the Morris Traveller had arrived on the scene. It seems to be a busy day at the Shire Hall - home to the county's court-hearings - judging by the number of people gathered outside.

◀ **Chelmsford High Street 1892** 31508
The central feature here - the stone rotunda standing at Springfield Road corner - had previously marked the conduit-head in Tindal Square. A conduit was established there in the Middle Ages, possibly by Chelmsford's house of friars. It tapped the water from the Burgess Well (now under Fairfield Road car park) and released it in an open channel down the High Street.

the
QUEENS
HEAD
INN
PRINTING OFFICE

Chelmsford High Street 1895

35514

A busy day. Barnard's upholsterers - agents for the Ipswich Boot & Shoe Warehouse - occupied the site of the Black Boy, Chelmsford's once-famous coaching-inn. It had also served as the town's post office, but was rapidly killed-off by the advent of the railway. Dickens is known to have stopped-over there, one wet weekend in January 1835.

Music
Records
Singer Sewing Machines
Arms
Clarke's
Printing
Works

Chelmsford High Street 1919
69010
Cars and bicycles had replaced handcarts and drays: that is a Morris Oxford outside the hotel. There was even a shop selling gramophone records - C E Rippon, piano-tuner and harmonium-maker. J H Clarke's - seen here with its in-house printing works - remains an important bookseller and stationer in Chelmsford to this day.

Chelmsford, High Street 1898 41504
A major photo opportunity. Barnard's, as well as its more secular functions, was also a temperance hotel: there were several of these in Chelmsford. Evidently Barnard's needed some work done on its roof. The old Conduit was now settling into its new role as lamp standard cum traffic island.

Chelmsford, High Street c1955 C73031
Familiar high street names were putting in an appearance: Marks & Spencer and Halford's Cycle & Motor Store. Bond's was a department store – 'The House For Value and Distinctive Ideas'. It was justly proud of its restaurant (advertised on the banner), as it was a stylish and popular meeting-place.

Chelmsford, High Street c1965 C73068

This view is from the island of shops separating the High Street and Tindal Street - or Fore Street and Back Street as they were anciently known. The island began life in the Middle Ages as a row of market stalls which gradually became permanent fixtures. The vehicle nearest the camera is a delivery van for Dunmow Flitch, the bacon company.

Chelmsford High Street 1919

69011

Of interest here are the two (separate) shops on the right-hand side: Wenley Ltd, and Bolingbroke & Sons. The former sold carpets, wallpaper and timber; the latter dealt in drapery. They traded next door to each other for decades before merging in 1967. Wenley's was the first Chelmsford shop to install a lift.

Chelmsford, High Street c1955 C73044
The Temperance Hotel had given way to Boot's. Also gone was the old Conduit: it was moved in 1939 to Tower Gardens. A more functional traffic island had replaced it and the age of the zebra crossing was under way. So, too, was another age: see the Curry's Television van parked in front of the Queen's Head.

Chelmsford, High Street c1965 C73067
Bond's - its name in chunky 1960s lettering - is here designated 'A Debenham Store'. During the 70s it became simply Debenham's. Woolworth's, Burton Tailoring and Tesco are among the other names visible here. Missing, of course, is the enormous Cater House - though the crane indicates that it was already more than a twinkle in the architect's eye.

Chelmsford Tindal Street 1906 56882
Ask a Chelmsfordian to name the biggest planning crime in the town's history, and the chances are that they will mention the demolition of Tindal Street in 1969-71. It contained a good many timber-framed and Georgian buildings, including a number of inns (up to 11 at one point). Notice that one of them, the White Hart, already boasted a public telephone.

W.PULHAM

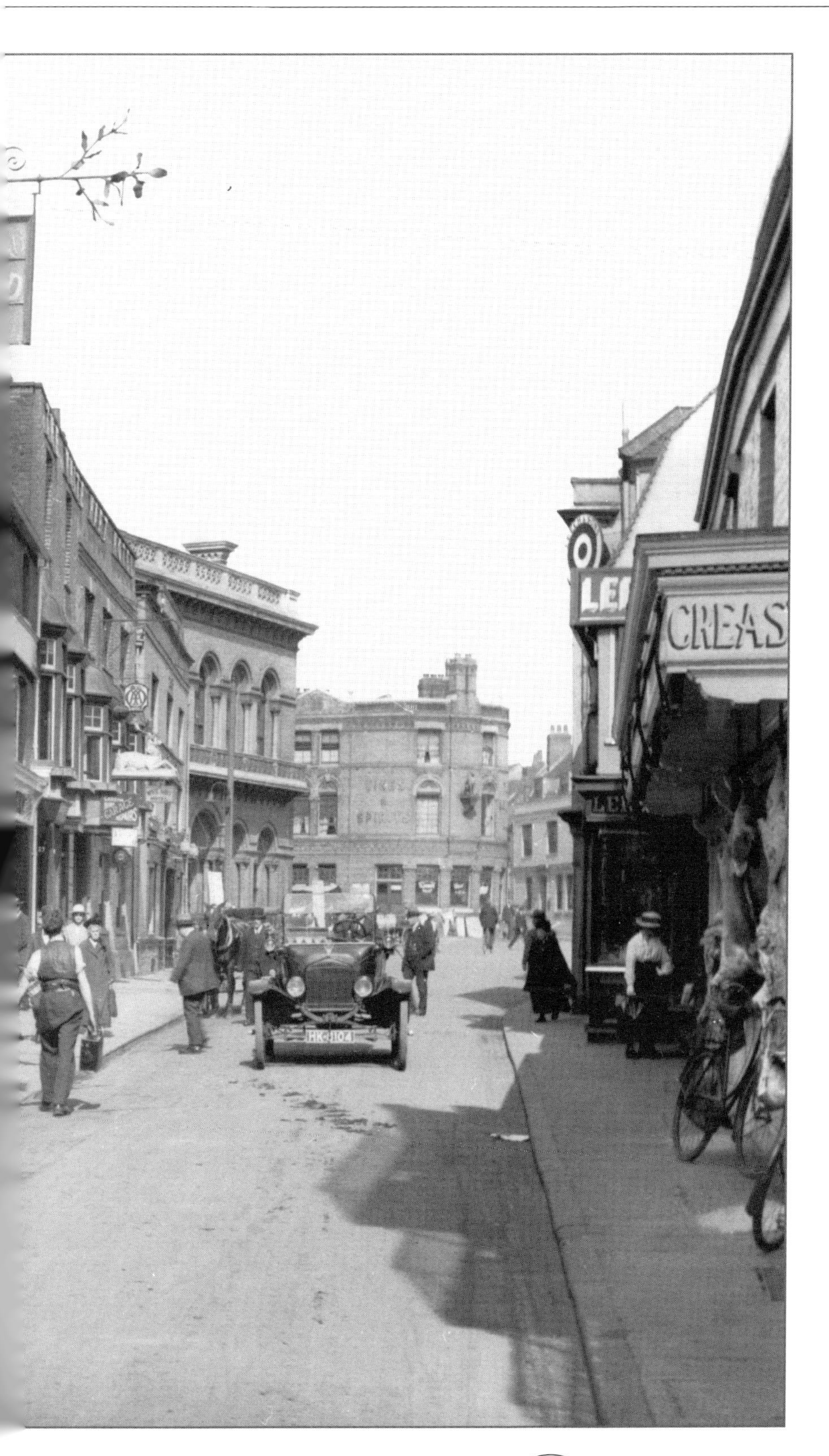

Chelmsford, Tindal Street 1919 69016
This photo encapsulates Tindal Street's higgledy-piggledy nature: the Spotted Dog's ornate bracket, the carcasses hanging outside Creasy's, and the target sign representing Leech the gunsmith's (est 1795). The balustraded building at the street's end is the Corn Exchange. After the decline of the agricultural industry, it became a dance hall. Notice how the lady walking past the entrance to the Spotted Dog's courtyard is still sticking rigidly to pre-War fashions.

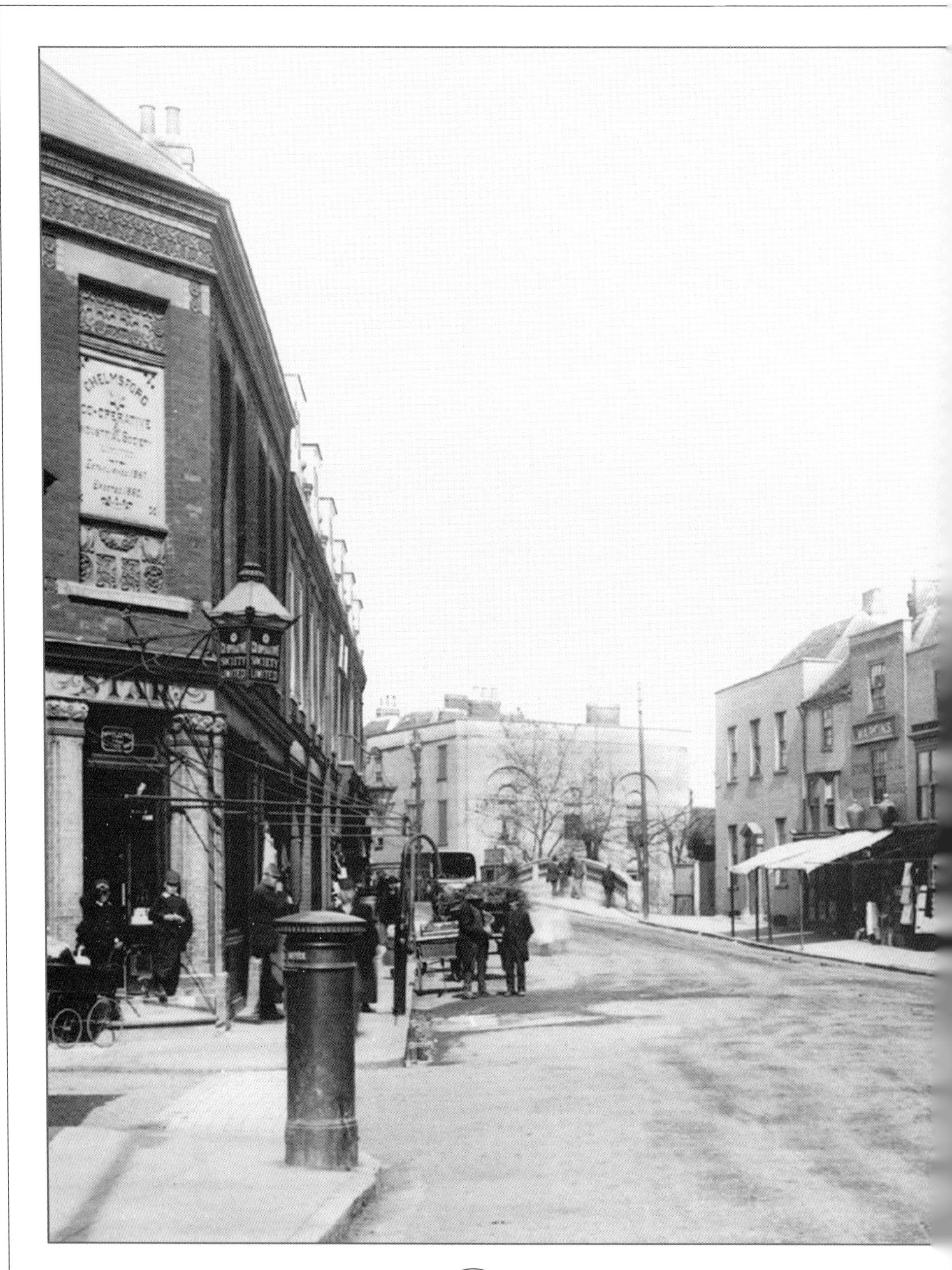
CHELMSFORD
CO-OPERATIVE
SOCIETY LIMITED

South of the Can: Moulsham

Chelmsford, Moulsham Street 1892 31509
The attractive half-timbered building is the Cross Keys, which was demolished in 1912. Three doors along from it is J G Bond's ('Milliner: Mantles and Dresses'), a branch of the department store in the High Street. Notice, further towards the bridge, Martin's Oil Stores using two large oil-jars as a trade-sign. The Star Co-op, on the left, occupied the site of Chelmsford's original gaol. It is still there today.

▼ **Chelmsford, Moulsham Street 1919** 69018

Pubs were vanishing. The octagonal tower is that of the Wesleyan church, which had replaced the Old Cock Inn. Over to the right, the Cross Keys had been superseded by the Regent Theatre. Chelmsford was considered something of a theatre-loving town at this time. Opposite - a sign of the post-Great War years: a Ministry of Labour Employment Exchange.

▼ **Chelmsford, The Wesleyan Church 1898** 41505

Photographed in the year it was built, this church had seating for 800 people, and a commodious schoolroom at the back. The latter was linked to the main building by a bridge across the Gullet - a small channel connecting the Rivers Chelmer and Can. The church was later replaced by the skyscraping Cater House.

▲ **Chelmsford Moulsham Street 1919** 69019

A conspicuously clean-looking street scene with only the faintest trace of horses. Loveday & Sons, the jewellers, have now occupied their shop at Baddow Road corner for over a century. Wright's Art Shop is an interesting addition: maybe it was intended to catch the eye of the theatre-going classes. Foster's, meanwhile, were making lofty claims: perhaps the proximity of Bond's and Rankin's was simply prompting an atmosphere of healthy competition.

◄ **Chelmsford Moulsham Street c1950** C73028

A busy shopping day, at a time before Moulsham Street was effectively bisected by Chelmsford's inner relief road. Baddow Road, on the left, was still the main through-route to Southend. Notice the ratio of bicycles to motor vehicles, even at this date. Moulsham Street was the original Roman road from London.

WINDMILL
FINE
ALES

Chelmsford Moulsham Street 1919 69020

The cluster of timber-framed buildings on the right were known as the Friars, having once abutted onto the gatehouse of Chelmsford's Dominican friary. The friary itself had steadily collapsed after the Dissolution, and these last remnants were dismantled in 1931. Among other things, the friary had been the early home of King Edward VI Grammar School. Across the road hangs the distinctive sign of Hindmarsh the pawnbroker. This area now lies under Parkway.

Chelmsford, The Stone Bridge 1919 69031
The Stone Bridge over the River Can - otherwise Bishop's Bridge or Moulsham Bridge - is the primeval hub of Chelmsford. There was probably a bridge here in Roman times. The current one was built in 1787 by John Johnson, County Surveyor, replacing a structure of 1372. South of the river, Chelmsford becomes Moulsham.

Chelmsford, The Stone Bridge 1892 31515
The property where the boys are standing is the Old Cock Inn. Six years later, it was cleared to make way for the Wesleyan church. On the far side of the bridge is Nichols & Jeffreys, who boasted 'A Large Stock of First Class Ready Made Clothing Equal to Bespoke … Style Fit & Durability Combined'.

Chelmsford, The Stone Bridge c1955 C73043
Foster's stood where Chelmsford's first gaol had stood. The gaol was demolished in 1859, and the site used as a parade ground by the West Essex Militia, hence the current street name Barrack Square. The polygonal building is the Congregational church, seen from behind. The Can, here, used to be called the Great River.

Chelmsford, The River Can 1906 56891
Museum Terrace, just to the left of the iron bridge in New London Road, was built in the 1840s. At various times it incorporated a boarding school, shops, private residences and - as the name suggests - the town's museum. Central Park now extends to the iron bridge. The warehouse in the distance was Wenley's carpet showroom.

▼ Chelmsford, The Stone Bridge 1919 69030

This view was taken from the iron bridge, and shows the backs of various High Street and Moulsham Street properties. Some of them had their own landing stages. The weather-boarded building - previously Wenley's - belonged, in 1919, to Hunt's the builders' merchants. There is no vegetation here now.

▼ Chelmsford, The Congregational Church 1906 56894

This church was built in 1840 by James Fenton, a leading engineer and nonconformist. It could accommodate up to 2,000 people. By the time of its demolition in 1971, the congregation had amalgamated with that of Baddow Road Congregational Church and built the new Christ Church on the site of a former brickyard in New London Road.

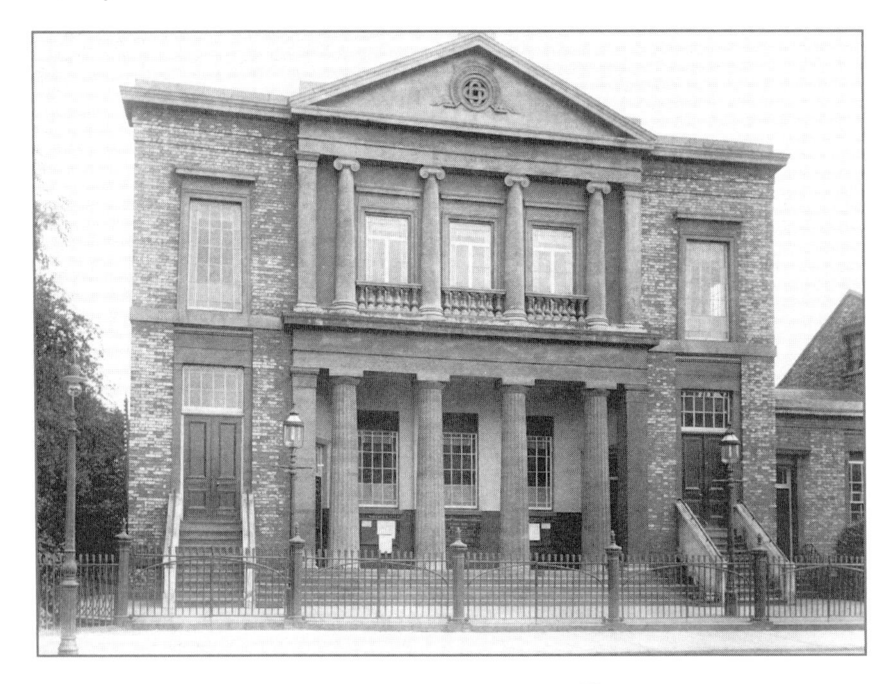

▲ Chelmsford The Congregational Church 1895 35524

The bridge on which the boys are standing was relatively new when this photo was taken. It was built in 1890 to replace an earlier iron bridge which had been swept away in the Great Flood of August 1888. The town has always been particularly susceptible to flooding. A prevention scheme was introduced in the 1960s.

◄ **Chelmsford**
The Infirmary 1895

35525

A Free Dispensary for the poor had been set up at the rear of the churchyard in 1818, but there was an increasing need for better facilities, and the Infirmary & Dispensary was built in New London Road in 1883. It was funded by public subscription, and a tablet of contributors' names can still be seen inside the porch.

Chelmsford, The Infirmary 1892 31514
In 1839 an amount of farmland (previously belonging to the Mildmay family) was sold to developers. It became New London Road - Moulsham Street being the 'old' London Road. The developers were staunch nonconformists, and here we can see the Ebenezer Strict Baptist Chapel just to the right of the Infirmary.

Chelmsford, The Hospital 1919 69033
The Infirmary (on the right) was built opposite Coleman & Morton's ironworks - a firm that had specialised in ploughs and cultivators, but closed as a result of the agricultural depression. A skating-rink had appeared on the site by 1919. The Infirmary - by then Chelmsford & Essex Hospital - closed its wards and most of its departments in the late 1980s. Its frontage is a protected building and still stands, housing a small range of health services.

Chelmsford, The Roman Catholic Church 1925 78166
In 1847, the Church of the Immaculate Conception was opened in New London Road. It was financed by local benefactors - some of them commemorated in the church's stained-glass windows. It was Chelmsford's first purpose-built Catholic church, although a building at the Wood Street Barracks had been used for RC worship during the Napoleonic Wars.

Chelmsford, Mildmay Road 1906 56886
We are standing at the corner of Lady Lane, looking east. It is a road of late Victorian houses with names like Pretoria Villas, Rebecca Place and Grasmere. The newly-erected telegraph lines suggest the relative affluence of this street. Other than the small child posing with its nanny, everywhere looks extremely quiet, too.

Chelmsford, St John's Church 1892 31512
St John's was built in 1837 on the site of a hop-garden. Even today, there is a stretch of the churchyard wall that appears to pre-date the church itself, and looks as if it should enclose a garden. Moulsham had never had its own church before, having been simply a hamlet in the parish of Chelmsford. In the 1880s it also acquired a church school - just visible on the left. Nowadays, St John's is still very much the dominant feature on Moulsham's skyline.

Park Life

Chelmsford
The Recreation Ground 1895 35518
The Bathing Pond (later just known as the Lake) was first created in the 1840s: it was the pit left after enough earth had been dug to make the railway embankment. The viaduct, completed in September 1842, consists of 18 arches. It took shape at a rate of 80,600 bricks per day.

Chelmsford
The Recreation Ground 1895 35522
The 'Rec' - now Central Park - was opened in 1894. Pathways were laid out and small landing stages constructed. The willow-trees were pollarded every five years to provide fencing materials. The young girl's boater and pinafore are typical of the period.

Chelmsford
The Recreation Ground 1895 35523
This part of the Rec, known as Bell Meadow, was a world of flower-beds, rustic bridges, arbours, and people strolling with parasols. The building with its back to us is the Literary & Mechanics Institute, a kind of forerunner of an adult education centre. By the date of this photo, however, it was already on the wane, and closed four years later.

Chelmsford
The Recreation Ground 1901 46728
The River Can, as seen from the rustic bridge, pursues a winding course. The distant buildings were part of the Cattle Market, which had occupied the site since 1880 - its place now taken, ironically, by Chelmsford's deeply unattractive covered market. Parkway now crosses this view where the river bends.

Chelmsford
The Recreation Ground, The Lake 1919 69036
With the decadent 1920s in the air, skirts were getting shorter - even for middle-aged ladies. As for the Lake, it had been rather superseded as a bathing facility when the town's outdoor swimming pool opened in Waterloo Lane in 1906. The Lake came into its own as the domain of fishermen and young courting couples.

Chelmsford The Recreation Ground The Bowling Green 1906 56893

Park Road - on the right here - used to lead to the bandstand; it had been called Vineyard Road before the Rec opened. Bowls is still played in the park, although this particular green is now under Parkway. The bandstand was never the same after a bomb fell nearby during the Second World War, and it was demolished soon after.

Chelmsford, The Recreation Ground 1919 69037
Here, at the edge of the bowling green, are two vehicles standing in striking contrast: the doll's pram and the tank. The latter was a veteran of the recently-finished Great War - a standard Mk IV model. For the park's promenaders, there were refreshments available at the building on the right.

Chelmsford, Admiral's Park 1919 69035
Pre-dating the Rec, Admiral's Park was once the residence of John Faithful Fortescue, a rear-admiral who died in 1820. Today, the two parks are connected by a pleasant footpath/cycle path along the Can. This view has not changed significantly, although the trees look a little less majestic now.

Chelmsford, Admiral's Park 1919 69034
This bridge no longer exists, but its old piles are still there. This stretch of the river is pleasantly overgrown in summer. Before Chelmsford acquired its recreation grounds, outdoor leisure activities had tended to centre upon the cricket ground in New Street, or the Fair Field (where the bus-station now stands).

Chelmsford, Tower Gardens 1925 78161
The Gardens took their name from a water tower that formerly stood here. Today they accommodate cricket pitches, a bowling green and formal gardens, as well as tennis. Since 1939, Tower Gardens have also been home to the former Conduit, after its removal from Springfield Road corner. It now stands on the left, where the shelter was.

Surrounding Villages: East and South

Springfield, The Mill 1906 56906
The River Chelmer now lends its name to the Riverside Leisure Centre, which stands on the near bank, behind the photographer. There had been a mill here for centuries. It still stands, though these days it is the Riverside Inn. There is a preservation order on it, and at one time there had even been talk of it becoming a museum.

▼ **Springfield, Holy Trinity Church 1898** 41506
Springfield had started to grow after the canal-basin arrived here. Holy Trinity was built in 1843 as a chapel of ease for the expanding population. Its neo-Norman style - complete with round-headed arches and corbel tables - was very much of its time. The triangle beneath the bellcote symbolizes the Trinity itself. This is still a surprisingly peaceful place.

▼ **Springfield, Holy Trinity Church 1906** 56907
The churchyard contains a memorial to Emily Gage, aged 19, "who gave her life 2 May 1844 in effort to save Mary McHandy from drowning in the River Chelmer". Mary could not be saved, and died, aged 11. Her father, John McHandy, was the Chief Constable of Essex.

▲ **Springfield, Lawn Lan 1906** 56904
This was a very rural thoroughfare until after the Second World War. The small boy's sailor sui was typical of the Edwardian period; as were the white skirts, worn only a couple of inches from the surface of the dirt road. There is now suburban infill on both sides of the lane.

◄ **Springfield, The Church 1892** 31517

All Saints' church, admired for its brick tower, has a nave dating back to the 12th century. Notice, on the green, the large-wheeled pram and, further to the right, the more primitive three-wheeled baby carriage. This was already a fairly antiquated design when the picture was taken.

Springfield, The Place 1906 56905
This early 18th century house was once the home of John Strutt, who owned the mills at Moulsham and Springfield. A more unseemly occupant is 'the squat figure of a man', who has haunted the building at various points in its history: the last sighting was in the 1940s, when Hoffmans were using the Place as a hostel for their workers.

Springfield, Baddow Meads 1919 69032
In the 1790s, after much deliberation, the Chelmer was canalised between Chelmsford and Maldon. This particular bend of the river was bypassed - note the absence of towpaths on either side. We are not far from Sandford Mill here: a view which, despite its proximity to the ever-expanding Chelmer Village, has so far escaped development.

Little Baddow, Grace's Walk 1903 50243
Named after the Le Gras family, Grace's Walk is a mile-long avenue of trees leading to Great Graces - a medieval mansion that has gently evolved into a farmhouse. Pointing westwards, Grace's Walk seems to make a beeline for the spire of Chelmsford Cathedral.

Little Baddow, Grace's Walk 1906 56895
This point - where Grace's Walk crosses Sandon Brook - has a ghost story attached to it: Lady Alice Mildmay (d1615), child-bride of Sir Henry, supposedly drowned herself in a pond here after he was unkind to her. It is likely the tale was invented - or at least embellished - by Jesse Berridge, who was rector of Little Baddow from 1915 to 1947. He used it as the basis for a novel entitled 'Gracy's Walk'.

Little Baddow
The Thatched Cottage
1903 50244
Riffhams Chase was, at this time, still a private road. It was barred from the outside world by a gate - seen here beside the Thatched Cottage. The fields at the rear of the cottage served as a parade ground for troops stationed in the village during the First World War. It was later a sports field.

Little Baddow, Riffhams Chase 1906 56896
Judging by the number of her appearances, this young model was being kept busy in 1906. The manor of Riffhams was centred upon Old Riffhams - a house which was at one point occupied by one Charles Smoothy. A keen ornithologist and taxidermist, it is his collection of birds that can still be seen in the Chelmsford & Essex Museum.

Little Baddow, The Post Office and North Hill c1960 L153009
The Post Office had occupied these premises since the 1930s. The brick building on the other side of the road was the school, which had been in the adjacent white house until 1851. Benjamin Horth, the then headmaster, was also the village postman. Before the Education Act, pupils paid 1d a week to attend.

Little Baddow, The Rodney 1903 50242
The Rodney is a pub with a tangled history. In fact, it has been two pubs with the same name. The one in the photo is the 'Old' Rodney, which in turn gave its name to the 16 acres of brake and heather in the foreground (now Heather Hills). A pleasure garden was established here in 1885 by one Elijah Mecklenberg.

Little Baddow, Paper Mill Lock, The River Chelmer c1960 L153011
Of the 11 locks on the Chelmer & Blackwater Navigation, this is something of a halfway house. It stands just upstream of the road to Hatfield Peverel, in an area sometimes known as World's End. The last mill burned down in 1905, though at one point there had been two mills here - one paper, one wheat. Coal, timber, lime and dung were the other major cargoes passing through. The road bridge was built in 1935.

▼ **Danbury, The Village, Looking East 1903** 50236
Danbury sits at the top of a long uphill haul on the road from Chelmsford to Maldon. Before the Navigation was opened, this was the main thoroughfare between the two towns. The low wall on the extreme left had been a pound - an overnight stopping-point for animals being driven to Chelmsford's livestock market.

▼ **Danbury, The Griffin Hotel 1903** 50238
Formerly a farmhouse, the Griffin first appears as an inn in 1744. It contains some 15th century woodcarvings from Danbury church - as well as some wall-stencilling identical to that in the church - and oak beams that came from a ship. It is even alleged to have a secret room. Sir Walter Scott is known to have stayed at the Griffin, and he named it in the introduction to one of his novels.

▲ **Danbury, The Village Looking West 1903**
50235
Although not the highest point in Essex, Danbury certainly commands an impressive position. Drivers of vehicles such as the gig in the foreground, not only had the gradient to contend with, but also the uneven road surface. It would certainly have been a challenge for the early cycle clubs who met here in the late 19th century.

◄ **Danbury, The Church 1906** 56898

St John the Baptist's stands inside the earthworks of a Danish settlement. In 1779 a leaden coffin was dug from under the floor in the north aisle. It contained the well-preserved body of a medieval knight - immersed, said one observer, "in a liquor ... resembling mushroom catchup". The coffin was re-sealed and buried.

Woodham Walter
The Village 1903
50246
The two buildings nearest the camera - Wingtons and Bannister Cottage - are still there, but the other houses have been replaced. Gone, too, is the recumbent dog, though in 1903 he seemed to be the focus of much attention. Woodham Walter's well-known Tudor pub, the Bell, stands just out of the picture to the left.

East Hanningfield, The Windmill c1960 E255010
The Southend road separates East Hanningfield from its namesakes, West and South, and from the enormous Hanningfield Reservoir. At its centre, the village straddles the Tye (a much-used Essex word for 'green'). The Windmill is little changed, apart from the absence of its two front bays - their place taken by a small beer-garden.

East Hanningfield, The Post Office c1960 E255001
A very rural Post Office - part cottage, part shop. Note the Victorian post box and the arrow for the Telegraph Office. Telegrams were still a popular form of communication, but they were on their way out: for many people, they had always had a macabre association - having been bringers, frequently, of bad news during the War years.

Great Baddow, The Church 1898 41508
Once described as "one of the handsomest villages in Essex", Great Baddow just about retains some 'villageness', though it has been joined to Chelmsford for a long time. St Mary's is justly famous for its Tudor-brick clerestory, complete with its ornamental diaper-work (criss-cross patterning).

Galleywood, The White Bear c1965 G90016
The mini-skirt had arrived in Galleywood. Fifteen years earlier, this scene would have looked very different: the houses and shops on the right were still open farmland. Barrett's General Stores had previously been Mr and Mrs Johnson's fish and chip shop. Both the shop and the hip-roofed cottage to the right have now gone. The main street, Watchhouse Road, may have taken its name from a lookout camp here at the time of the Napoleonic Wars.

Surrounding Villages: West and North

Blackmore
The Bull c1955 B320002
Blackmore has always been a village of contrasts: this scene includes a modern double-decker bus and a Ford Popular. It also combines 20th century housing with the late 15th century Bull. The lane to the right of the pub is called Little Jordan - a punning reference to Blackmore's most famous building, Jericho Priory.

Blackmore, The Village c1955 B320009

Blackmore - seven miles from Chelmsford - is centred on Horsefayre Green, the small circular area on the right. It is a village well supplied with pubs: here we see the Leather Bottle, with its sign behind the tree, and the Prince Albert across the road. The shop has now reverted to domestic use.

Writtle, The Church 1898 41507

In 1800, shortly after the roof of Chelmsford's future cathedral had collapsed, the tower of All Saints', Writtle, followed suit. The events prompted the bucolic rhyme "Chelmsford church and Writtle steeple both fell down, but killed no people". Two years later, Writtle's belfry was "rebuilt after a tasteless fashion" ('Little Guide to Essex').

Writtle, Aubyns and the Church c1955 W154013
The tower had undergone a little more architectural tweaking by this time - though the church was to be damaged by fires in 1974 and 1991. Aubyns, in front of it, was built c1500. Writtle had been a market town before Chelmsford was: it presented an easier crossing-point over the Can once Chelmsford's Roman bridge had collapsed.

Writtle, The Village c1955 W154009
The duck pond on Writtle Green is still the jewel in this village's crown - though these days it has rails around it. It is interesting to note that the car in the middle of the photograph is a pre-War model: a common sight until the British motor industry picked up in the late 50s.

Writtle
The Green and Cottages c1955 W154017
This corner of Writtle has not altered: the pump and its attendant cottages are still there. The house to the right was originally a maltings - the structure with the lantern having been the oast-house. It belonged to the Writtle Brewery Company until they were taken over by Trumans. It also contains timbers from the dismantled Lordship Hunting Lodge.

Widford, The Church 1898 41509
Widford ('willow ford') was finally swallowed by Chelmsford in 1935. St Mary's church had been totally rebuilt in the 19th century. It still commands an imposing position, though the field in the foreground is now bisected by Writtle Bypass - and, behind the viewer, the Robjohns industrial estate has sprung up.

Roxwell, St Michael's Church 1967 R228013
Although basically medieval, St Michael's was ruthlessly restored by the Victorians. Masonry from the original windows was built into the churchyard wall. Francis Quarles, the Jacobean poet, lived at Roxwell for the last decade of his life: four of his 18 children were baptised in the parish church.

Roxwell, The Street c1965 R228015
The latter part of the village's name seems to be associated with a spring next to the churchyard. These weather-boarded cottages, opposite the church, are very 'Essex'. It has been suggested that weatherboarding may have been introduced to sidestep a tax on bricks - but this may be apocryphal.

▼ **Pleshey, The Village c1965** P146003
Pleshey's name means 'enclosure'. The village is, indeed, enclosed by a circular, pre-Roman ditch. In the 12th century a castle-keep was added, built on a central mount (hence the Mount Stores on the left). Pleshey's curving roads generally follow the concentric lines of the castle's ramparts.

▼ **Pleshey, The View From The Church Tower c1965** P146010
Pleshey's church dates only from 1868, though an earlier one had stood in the field behind the White Horse, on the left of the picture. The castle here had fallen into decay by Shakespeare's time: in 'Richard II', he mentions its "empty lodgings and unfurnished walls, unpeopled offices, untrodden stones". Evidently, it was already a byword for faded grandeur. Today, the mount - seen here on the right - has long been bare.

▲ **Great Waltham Chelmsford Road c1965** G101005
The Mini van heralds the height of the 'swinging 60s'. Next to the Post Office, Snow's the butchers were well-known for their Piggy Porker Sausages and, indeed, used to advertise them on the side of their delivery-van. This delicacy probably went down well with Vitbe. Snow's is now a house called, appropriately, No 1 Snows Court.

◀ **Great Waltham Chelmsford Road c1965**
G101009
We are standing on the small brick-parapeted bridge over the Walthambury Brook. Today, this view is largely unchanged, though the Regent Gaiage has been swept away, along with the Green Shield stamps it offered. Philip Morant, the Essex historian, was curate of Great Waltham 1724-32.

Little Waltham, The Village c1965 L158001
Little Waltham stood on the Chelmsford-Braintree road until it was bypassed in 1971. Even so, the village does not seem unduly troubled by traffic in this picture. The White Hart looks every inch the Georgian coaching-inn. It still holds its own today, although it has lost its wiggly ornamental bracket and projecting canopy.

Little Waltham, The Village c1965 L158008
We are standing on Winckford Bridge across the Chelmer - described by Peter Muilman in his 1769 'History of Essex' as "a handsome bridge built of wood, painted." Today, this scene is much as it was in 1965 - except that the production of 'Oklahoma!' has long since finished. Unlike 'The Mousetrap', it has not run and run.

Index

Chelmsford

Around Chelmsford

Frith Book Co Titles

www.francisfrith.co.uk

The Frith Book Company publishes over 100 new titles each year. A selection of those currently available are listed below. For latest catalogue please contact Frith Book Co.

Town Books 96pages, approx 100 photos. County and Themed Books 128pages, approx 150 photos (unless specified). All titles hardback laminated case and jacket except those indicated pb (paperback)

Amersham, Chesham & Rickmansworth (pb)	1-85937-340-2	£9.99
Ancient Monuments & Stone Circles	1-85937-143-4	£17.99
Aylesbury (pb)	1-85937-227-9	£9.99
Bakewell	1-85937-113-2	£12.99
Barnstaple (pb)	1-85937-300-3	£9.99
Bath (pb)	1-85937419-0	£9.99
Bedford (pb)	1-85937-205-8	£9.99
Berkshire (pb)	1-85937-191-4	£9.99
Berkshire Churches	1-85937-170-1	£17.99
Blackpool (pb)	1-85937-382-8	£9.99
Bognor Regis (pb)	1-85937-431-x	£9.99
Bournemouth	1-85937-067-5	£12.99
Bradford (pb)	1-85937-204-x	£9.99
Brighton & Hove(pb)	1-85937-192-2	£8.99
Bristol (pb)	1-85937-264-3	£9.99
British Life A Century Ago (pb)	1-85937-213-9	£9.99
Buckinghamshire (pb)	1-85937-200-7	£9.99
Camberley (pb)	1-85937-222-8	£9.99
Cambridge (pb)	1-85937-422-0	£9.99
Cambridgeshire (pb)	1-85937-420-4	£9.99
Canals & Waterways (pb)	1-85937-291-0	£9.99
Canterbury Cathedral (pb)	1-85937-179-5	£9.99
Cardiff (pb)	1-85937-093-4	£9.99
Carmarthenshire	1-85937-216-3	£14.99
Chelmsford (pb)	1-85937-310-0	£9.99
Cheltenham (pb)	1-85937-095-0	£9.99
Cheshire (pb)	1-85937-271-6	£9.99
Chester	1-85937-090-x	£12.99
Chesterfield	1-85937-378-x	£9.99
Chichester (pb)	1-85937-228-7	£9.99
Colchester (pb)	1-85937-188-4	£8.99
Cornish Coast	1-85937-163-9	£14.99
Cornwall (pb)	1-85937-229-5	£9.99
Cornwall Living Memories	1-85937-248-1	£14.99
Cotswolds (pb)	1-85937-230-9	£9.99
Cotswolds Living Memories	1-85937-255-4	£14.99
County Durham	1-85937-123-x	£14.99
Croydon Living Memories	1-85937-162-0	£9.99
Cumbria	1-85937-101-9	£14.99
Dartmoor	1-85937-145-0	£14.99
Derby (pb)	1-85937-367-4	£9.99
Derbyshire (pb)	1-85937-196-5	£9.99
Devon (pb)	1-85937-297-x	£9.99
Dorset (pb)	1-85937-269-4	£9.99
Dorset Churches	1-85937-172-8	£17.99
Dorset Coast (pb)	1-85937-299-6	£9.99
Dorset Living Memories	1-85937-210-4	£14.99
Down the Severn	1-85937-118-3	£14.99
Down the Thames (pb)	1-85937-278-3	£9.99
Down the Trent	1-85937-311-9	£14.99
Dublin (pb)	1-85937-231-7	£9.99
East Anglia (pb)	1-85937-265-1	£9.99
East London	1-85937-080-2	£14.99
East Sussex	1-85937-130-2	£14.99
Eastbourne	1-85937-061-6	£12.99
Edinburgh (pb)	1-85937-193-0	£8.99
England in the 1880's	1-85937-331-3	£17.99
English Castles (pb)	1-85937-434-4	£9.99
English Country Houses	1-85937-161-2	£17.99
Essex (pb)	1-85937-270-8	£9.99
Exeter	1-85937-126-4	£12.99
Exmoor	1-85937-132-9	£14.99
Falmouth	1-85937-066-7	£12.99
Folkestone (pb)	1-85937-124-8	£9.99
Glasgow (pb)	1-85937-190-6	£9.99
Gloucestershire	1-85937-102-7	£14.99
Great Yarmouth (pb)	1-85937-426-3	£9.99
Greater Manchester (pb)	1-85937-266-x	£9.99
Guildford (pb)	1-85937-410-7	£9.99
Hampshire (pb)	1-85937-279-1	£9.99
Hampshire Churches (pb)	1-85937-207-4	£9.99
Harrogate	1-85937-423-9	£9.99
Hastings & Bexhill (pb)	1-85937-131-0	£9.99
Heart of Lancashire (pb)	1-85937-197-3	£9.99
Helston (pb)	1-85937-214-7	£9.99
Hereford (pb)	1-85937-175-2	£9.99
Herefordshire	1-85937-174-4	£14.99
Hertfordshire (pb)	1-85937-247-3	£9.99
Horsham (pb)	1-85937-432-8	£9.99
Humberside	1-85937-215-5	£14.99
Hythe, Romney Marsh & Ashford	1-85937-256-2	£9.99
Ipswich (pb)	1-85937-424-7	£9.99
Ireland (pb)	1-85937-181-7	£9.99
Isle of Man (pb)	1-85937-268-6	£9.99
Isles of Scilly	1-85937-136-1	£14.99
Isle of Wight (pb)	1-85937-429-8	£9.99
Isle of Wight Living Memories	1-85937-304-6	£14.99
Kent (pb)	1-85937-189-2	£9.99

Available from your local bookshop or from the publisher

Frith Book Co Titles (continued)

Kent Living Memories	1-85937-125-6	£14.99
Lake District (pb)	1-85937-275-9	£9.99
Lancaster, Morecambe & Heysham (pb)	1-85937-233-3	£9.99
Leeds (pb)	1-85937-202-3	£9.99
Leicester	1-85937-073-x	£12.99
Leicestershire (pb)	1-85937-185-x	£9.99
Lighthouses	1-85937-257-0	£17.99
Lincolnshire (pb)	1-85937-433-6	£9.99
Liverpool & Merseyside (pb)	1-85937-234-1	£9.99
London (pb)	1-85937-183-3	£9.99
Ludlow (pb)	1-85937-176-0	£9.99
Luton (pb)	1-85937-235-x	£9.99
Maidstone	1-85937-056-x	£14.99
Manchester (pb)	1-85937-198-1	£9.99
Middlesex	1-85937-158-2	£14.99
New Forest	1-85937-128-0	£14.99
Newark (pb)	1-85937-366-6	£9.99
Newport, Wales (pb)	1-85937-258-9	£9.99
Newquay (pb)	1-85937-421-2	£9.99
Norfolk (pb)	1-85937-195-7	£9.99
Norfolk Living Memories	1-85937-217-1	£14.99
Northamptonshire	1-85937-150-7	£14.99
Northumberland Tyne & Wear (pb)	1-85937-281-3	£9.99
North Devon Coast	1-85937-146-9	£14.99
North Devon Living Memories	1-85937-261-9	£14.99
North London	1-85937-206-6	£14.99
North Wales (pb)	1-85937-298-8	£9.99
North Yorkshire (pb)	1-85937-236-8	£9.99
Norwich (pb)	1-85937-194-9	£8.99
Nottingham (pb)	1-85937-324-0	£9.99
Nottinghamshire (pb)	1-85937-187-6	£9.99
Oxford (pb)	1-85937-411-5	£9.99
Oxfordshire (pb)	1-85937-430-1	£9.99
Peak District (pb)	1-85937-280-5	£9.99
Penzance	1-85937-069-1	£12.99
Peterborough (pb)	1-85937-219-8	£9.99
Piers	1-85937-237-6	£17.99
Plymouth	1-85937-119-1	£12.99
Poole & Sandbanks (pb)	1-85937-251-1	£9.99
Preston (pb)	1-85937-212-0	£9.99
Reading (pb)	1-85937-238-4	£9.99
Romford (pb)	1-85937-319-4	£9.99
Salisbury (pb)	1-85937-239-2	£9.99
Scarborough (pb)	1-85937-379-8	£9.99
St ALbans (pb)	1-85937-341-0	£9.99
St Ives (pb)	1-85937415-8	£9.99
Scotland (pb)	1-85937-182-5	£9.99
Scottish Castles (pb)	1-85937-323-2	£9.99
Sevenoaks & Tunbridge	1-85937-057-8	£12.99
Sheffield, South Yorks (pb)	1-85937-267-8	£9.99
Shrewsbury (pb)	1-85937-325-9	£9.99
Shropshire (pb)	1-85937-326-7	£9.99
Somerset	1-85937-153-1	£14.99
South Devon Coast	1-85937-107-8	£14.99
South Devon Living Memories	1-85937-168-x	£14.99
South Hams	1-85937-220-1	£14.99
Southampton (pb)	1-85937-427-1	£9.99
Southport (pb)	1-85937-425-5	£9.99
Staffordshire	1-85937-047-0	£12.99
Stratford upon Avon	1-85937-098-5	£12.99
Suffolk (pb)	1-85937-221-x	£9.99
Suffolk Coast	1-85937-259-7	£14.99
Surrey (pb)	1-85937-240-6	£9.99
Sussex (pb)	1-85937-184-1	£9.99
Swansea (pb)	1-85937-167-1	£9.99
Tees Valley & Cleveland	1-85937-211-2	£14.99
Thanet (pb)	1-85937-116-7	£9.99
Tiverton (pb)	1-85937-178-7	£9.99
Torbay	1-85937-063-2	£12.99
Truro	1-85937-147-7	£12.99
Victorian and Edwardian Cornwall	1-85937-252-x	£14.99
Victorian & Edwardian Devon	1-85937-253-8	£14.99
Victorian & Edwardian Kent	1-85937-149-3	£14.99
Vic & Ed Maritime Album	1-85937-144-2	£17.99
Victorian and Edwardian Sussex	1-85937-157-4	£14.99
Victorian & Edwardian Yorkshire	1-85937-154-x	£14.99
Victorian Seaside	1-85937-159-0	£17.99
Villages of Devon (pb)	1-85937-293-7	£9.99
Villages of Kent (pb)	1-85937-294-5	£9.99
Villages of Sussex (pb)	1-85937-295-3	£9.99
Warwickshire (pb)	1-85937-203-1	£9.99
Welsh Castles (pb)	1-85937-322-4	£9.99
West Midlands (pb)	1-85937-289-9	£9.99
West Sussex	1-85937-148-5	£14.99
West Yorkshire (pb)	1-85937-201-5	£9.99
Weymouth (pb)	1-85937-209-0	£9.99
Wiltshire (pb)	1-85937-277-5	£9.99
Wiltshire Churches (pb)	1-85937-171-x	£9.99
Wiltshire Living Memories	1-85937-245-7	£14.99
Winchester (pb)	1-85937-428-x	£9.99
Windmills & Watermills	1-85937-242-2	£17.99
Worcester (pb)	1-85937-165-5	£9.99
Worcestershire	1-85937-152-3	£14.99
York (pb)	1-85937-199-x	£9.99
Yorkshire (pb)	1-85937-186-8	£9.99
Yorkshire Living Memories	1-85937-166-3	£14.99

See Frith books on the internet www.francisfrith.co.uk

FRITH PRODUCTS & SERVICES

Francis Frith would doubtless be pleased to know that the pioneering publishing venture he started in 1860 still continues today. A hundred and forty years later, The Francis Frith Collection continues in the same innovative tradition and is now one of the foremost publishers of vintage photographs in the world. Some of the current activities include:

Interior Decoration

Today Frith's photographs can be seen framed and as giant wall murals in thousands of pubs, restaurants, hotels, banks, retail stores and other public buildings throughout the country. In every case they enhance the unique local atmosphere of the places they depict and provide reminders of gentler days in an increasingly busy and frenetic world.

Product Promotions

Frith products are used by many major companies to promote the sales of their own products or to reinforce their own history and heritage. Frith promotions have been used by Hovis bread, Courage beers, Scots Porage Oats, Colman's mustard, Cadbury's foods, Mellow Birds coffee, Dunhill pipe tobacco, Guinness, and Bulmer's Cider.

Genealogy and Family History

As the interest in family history and roots grows world-wide, more and more people are turning to Frith's photographs of Great Britain for images of the towns, villages and streets where their ancestors lived; and, of course, photographs of the churches and chapels where their ancestors were christened, married and buried are an essential part of every genealogy tree and family album.

Frith Products

All Frith photographs are available Framed or just as Mounted Prints and Posters (size 23 x 16 inches). These may be ordered from the address below. From time to time other products - Address Books, Calendars, Table Mats, etc - are available.

The Internet

Already twenty thousand Frith photographs can be viewed and purchased on the internet through the Frith websites and a myriad of partner sites.

For more detailed information on Frith companies and products, look at these sites:

www.francisfrith.co.uk
www.francisfrith.com
(for North American visitors)

See the complete list of Frith Books at:
www.francisfrith.co.uk

This web site is regularly updated with the latest list of publications from the Frith Book Company. If you wish to buy books relating to another part of the country that your local bookshop does not stock, you may purchase on-line.

For further information, trade, or author enquiries please contact us at the address below:

The Francis Frith Collection, Frith's Barn, Teffont, Salisbury, Wiltshire, England SP3 5QP.
Tel: +44 (0)1722 716 376 Fax: +44 (0)1722 716 881 Email: sales@francisfrith.co.uk

TO RECEIVE YOUR FREE MOUNTED PRINT

Mounted Print
Overall size 14 x 11 inches

Cut out this Voucher and return it with your remittance for £1.95 to cover postage and handling, to UK addresses. For overseas addresses please include £4.00 post and handling.
Choose any photograph included in this book. Your SEPIA print will be A4 in size, and mounted in a cream mount with burgundy rule line, overall size 14 x 11 inches.

Order additional Mounted Prints at HALF PRICE (only £7.49 each*)
If there are further pictures you would like to order, possibly as gifts for friends and family, purchase them at half price (no additional postage and handling required).

Have your Mounted Prints framed*
For an additional £14.95 per print you can have your chosen Mounted Print framed in an elegant polished wood and gilt moulding, overall size 16 x 13 inches (no additional postage and handling required).

*** IMPORTANT!**
These special prices are only available if ordered using the original voucher on this page (no copies permitted) and at the same time as your free Mounted Print, for delivery to the same address

Frith Collectors' Guild

From time to time we publish a magazine of news and stories about Frith photographs and further special offers of Frith products. If you would like 12 months FREE membership, please return this form.

Send completed forms to:
The Francis Frith Collection, Frith's Barn, Teffont, Salisbury, Wiltshire SP3 5QP

Voucher for FREE and Reduced Price Frith Prints

Picture no.	Page number	Qty	Mounted @ £7.49	Framed + £14.95	Total Cost
		1	Free of charge*	£	£
			£7.49	£	£
			£7.49	£	£
			£7.49	£	£
			£7.49	£	£
			£7.49	£	£

Please allow 28 days for delivery — *** Post & handling** **£1.95**

Book Title .... **Total Order Cost** **£**

Please do not photocopy this voucher. Only the original is valid, so please cut it out and return it to us.

I enclose a cheque / postal order for £ ....
made payable to 'The Francis Frith Collection'
OR please debit my Mastercard / Visa / Switch / Amex card
(credit cards please on all overseas orders)

Number ....

Issue No (Switch only) .... Valid from (Amex/Switch) ....

Expires .... Signature ....

Name Mr/Mrs/Ms ....

Address ....

....

....

.... Postcode ....

Daytime Tel No .... Valid to 31/12/02

The Francis Frith Collectors' Guild

Please enrol me as a member for 12 months free of charge.

Name Mr/Mrs/Ms ....

Address ....

....

....

.... Postcode ....

Free Print - see overleaf

Would you like to find out more about Francis Frith?

We have recently recruited some entertaining speakers who are happy to visit local groups, clubs and societies to give an illustrated talk documenting Frith's travels and photographs. If you are a member of such a group and are interested in hosting a presentation, we would love to hear from you.

Our speakers bring with them a small selection of our local town and county books, together with sample prints. They are happy to take orders. A small proportion of the order value is donated to the group who have hosted the presentation. The talks are therefore an excellent way of fundraising for small groups and societies.

Can you help us with information about any of the Frith photographs in this book?

We are gradually compiling an historical record for each of the photographs in the Frith archive. It is always fascinating to find out the names of the people shown in the pictures, as well as insights into the shops, buildings and other features depicted.

If you recognize anyone in the photographs in this book, or if you have information not already included in the author's caption, do let us know. We would love to hear from you, and will try to publish it in future books or articles.

Our production team

Frith books are produced by a small dedicated team at offices in the converted Grade II listed 18th-century barn at Teffont near Salisbury, illustrated above. Most have worked with the Frith Collection for many years. All have in common one quality: they have a passion for the Frith Collection. The team is constantly expanding, but currently includes:

Jason Buck, John Buck, Douglas Burns, Heather Crisp, Isobel Hall, Rob Hames, Hazel Heaton, Peter Horne, James Kinnear, Tina Leary, Eliza Sackett, Terence Sackett, Sandra Sanger, Shelley Tolcher, Susanna Walker, Clive Wathen and Jenny Wathen.